Companion to the
Prayer of Christians

Companion to the *Prayer of Christians*

Reflections and Personal Prayers

John Burke, O.P.

A Liturgical Press Book

THE LITURGICAL PRESS
Collegeville, Minnesota

Cover design by David Manahan, O.S.B.

Excerpts taken from THE JERUSALEM BIBLE, published and © 1966, 1967, and 1968 by Darton Longman and Todd Ltd. and Doubleday & Co Inc., and used by permission of the publishers.

© 1995 by The Order of St. Benedict, Inc., Collegeville, Minnesota. All rights reserved. No part of this book may be reproduced in any form or by any means, electronic or mechanical, including photocopying, recording, taping, or any retrieval system, without the written permission of The Liturgical Press, Collegeville, Minnesota 56321. Printed in the United States of America.

1	2	3	4	5	6	7	8

Library of Congress Cataloging-in-Publication Data

Burke, John, 1928-
    Companion to the Prayer of Christians : reflections and personal prayers / John Burke.
      p.   cm.
    ISBN 0-8146-2097-3
    1. Catholic Church.   Liturgy of the hours.   2. Divine office.
I. Title.
BX2000.B87   1995
264'.0201—dc20   95-7429
                                                                CIP

CONTENTS

Introduction 7

Week I 17

Week II 33

Week III 48

Week IV 64

Psalms for Night Prayer 79

INTRODUCTION

Time

We are time-locked creatures. Time determines all of our functions and activities: the seasons affect our moods; the biological clock runs our bodies; schedules rule our lives. Time determines when we get up, when we go to work, when we can play, when to run errands, and when to sleep. Time's deadlines can be so demanding, and deadline-induced pressures can be so stressful, that we forget that time is a divine gift, meant to keep us close to God always. Time is a holy thing.

Offering the *Prayer of Christians* as personal daily prayer delivers Christians from the domination of time to the heartwarming experience of God's presence in all that they do throughout the entire day. The *Prayer of Christians*, also known as the Divine Office, is the official prayer of the Church Universal.

The Constitution on the Sacred Liturgy tells us that the Divine Office is laid out so that the whole course of the day and night is made holy by the praises of God. It goes on to say:

> When this wonderful song of praise is rightly performed, . . . it is the voice of the bride addressed to her bridegroom; it is the very prayer which Christ himself, together with his body addresses to the Father (CSL, no. 84).

Centered around the twin poles of morning and evening, the sacred beginning and the sacred end of each day, the *Prayer of Christians* brings together the entire Church in a common prayer of praise and thanksgiving. The Apostle Paul urges Christians:

> With gratitude in your hearts sing psalms and hymns and inspired songs to God, and never say or do anything except in the name of the Lord Jesus, giving thanks to God the Father through him (Col 3:16, 17).

Cosmic Prayer of Gifts

The Church Universal has existed for two thousand years in an amazing variety of cultures. Praying in communion with this Catholic Church delivers Christians today from a self-centered spirituality whose pious devotions are limited to asking for personal favors from God, sometimes desperately. The *Prayer of Christians* imparts a sense of the cosmic dimension of God's actions. It helps us recognize the gifts God has already given us, gifts that transcend time and space. The experience of oneness with the Church Universal is enhanced when the Divine Office is prayed aloud in common with fellow Christians, perhaps in the parish church.

The Apostle Paul invites us to praise God in the Letter to the Ephesians and inspires us by summing up God's gifts to us in one of the most beautiful passages in all of Sacred Scripture:

> Blessed be God the Father of our Lord Jesus Christ,
> who has blessed us with all the spiritual blessings of heaven in Christ.
> Before the world was made, he chose us, chose us in Christ,
> to be holy and spotless, and to live through love in his presence,

> determining that we should become his adopted children, through Jesus Christ
> for his own purposes,
> to make us praise the glory of his grace,
> his free gift to us in the Beloved,
> in whom, through his blood, we gain our freedom,
> the forgiveness of our sins (Eph 1:3-7).

God's Own Prayers

The *Prayer of Christians* uses God's own prayers—the divinely inspired psalms. The Old Testament Psalter evolved slowly: some psalms were written before the exile of the Jews to Babylon (587, 581 B.C.E.); some were written and added to the Psalter after the return from exile in 538 B.C.E. All together, they are the result of some seven hundred years of the Jewish experience of God.

More importantly, all this compiling, editing, and use in worship was the result of the guidance and inspiration of the Holy Spirit. The psalms that were admitted to the Sacred Canon of the Psalter are, therefore, the inspired word of God.

By proclaiming God's majesty and providence the psalms make us more and more conscious of God's infinite power, wisdom, and love. They define the promise given to those who live good lives in spite of suffering, and they reveal the disaster in store for those who do evil.

Praying the psalms inspires the Christian to delve more deeply into the entire Scriptures, God's own word. The Holy Bible reveals as no other book can our Father's guiding concern for all creatures, but especially for those who live in union with God's Son, Jesus Christ. As a result, no believer can pray the *Prayer of Christians* and not become optimistic about life—no matter how intense the suffering he or she must endure from time to time.

The Liturgical Cycle

At the same time, because the *Prayer of Christians* is in harmony with the liturgical cycle of the Church, praying this Holy Office incorporates us into the Church's yearly celebration of the great mysteries of Christ's birth, ministry, passion, death, and resurrection. Each Mass, each liturgical celebration, therefore, becomes a richer spiritual experience as our reading and praying of Scripture opens up a fresh and more fully developed understanding of what God has accomplished for us in Jesus Christ.

Cultic Prayers

The title of the Book of Psalms in Hebrew is *Tehillim*, which means "cultic songs of praise." They were sung to simple tunes that stressed rhythm to induce ecstasy and to accompany dance. Their emotive power comes from a poetic structure that is neither rhyme nor Western poetic meter. It is a rhythm of sense, not sound. The poetic force is based on parallelism: the repetition of images or ideas in two-line strophes.

Although some psalms had their origin as private poetry, others came into existence in connection with various cultic ceremonies. The rituals were frequently in the form of sacred dramas recalling God's saving action in the past and assuring the renewal of God's action in the future. The rite was, therefore, an eternal and recurring "now."

The celebration of Passover, for example, not only recalled the Exodus from Egypt to the Promised Land but also became the occasion wherein God, the worshipers believed, renewed the covenant with the chosen people.

The Holy Mass is a similar sacred drama, reenacting the Last Supper and making present once again the saving graces of Calvary. The sacraments, too, are powerful rites whose outward signs bestow the special graces of each sacrament. It must be clearly noted, however, that the sacraments of the New Testament, being sacraments of the Risen Christ and effecting the graces they signify, are substantially different from the rituals of the Old Testament.

Rites of Nature

In the Old Testament the psalms were used in the celebration of festivals intimately connected with nature: planting, waiting, harvesting, giving thanks for a bountiful harvest, calling on God to bless the New Year, asking for deliverance from drought. The ancients saw such rituals as power filled, world renewing, blessing bringing. The rites represented new life, and indeed the worshipers believed that when properly done, the rites actually created new life.

Except for natural disasters of overwhelming magnitude, the cycles of nature for most contemporary Americans are merely inconveniences. It is hard for city folk to appreciate the cycles of nature, such as the disaster a drought brings or the abundance that adequate rain brings. But for the farmer even a short drought at the wrong time can spell ruin.

An Acquired Taste for Ancient Poetry

Few people read even modern poetry today; our American culture prefers straightforward, realistic prose. Our literature expresses emotions, of course, but in narrative or psychological terms rather than in the images and evocative language of either the Psalter or traditional Western poetry.

Psalms are poems. Poems arise from the innermost recesses of the human psyche. They sing of a reality that is personally experienced and deeply felt, depicting it with lively imagination. Those who are praying the psalms for the first time may think that the same ideas and emotions are being repeated over and over to such an extent that they become bored, lose interest, and drop out. As with all literature of great value, it takes time to acquire a taste for the psalms.

Although they share some common qualities, individual psalms are quite different; but we have to look a little more closely to see the differences and to appreciate the poignant and rousing sentiments they are expressing.

The best of the individual psalms have about them the quality of personal witness to pain and praise. When we have become sensitive to their nuances, the psalms show great variety and richness of expression. And to be perfectly honest, they are not equally likeable; some are better than others. But all in all, the fact is that the psalms really do connect with our own emotions and understanding of human life: its pains as well as its joys.

Our Emotions in the Psalms

In fact, the psalms purify every emotion we have ever had. Our daily emotional reactions to events and people, emotions that all human beings have felt at one time or another, form the basis of daily prayer: hatred, anger, fear, envy, discouragement, sorrow, hunger for justice, as well as thanksgiving, praise, joy, and peace.

The one who prays the *Prayer of Christians* no longer tries to hide his or her true feeling from God, to whom "everything is uncovered and open" (Heb 4:13) anyway. Rather, even the most harmful emotions can be expressed and, yes, made holy, since when we reflect on them prayerfully (using God's own prayers) God uses our emotions to bring us closer. We grow in our ability to appreciate and celebrate God's providential care and eternal wisdom precisely through our emotional experience of life.

Enthusiastic Worship

If we can envision the religious rites in which the psalms were first used we will better understand why the Church continues to use them today.

To appreciate their emotive power when praying the psalms, either by simply reciting them alone, or better, by chanting them with others, imagine throngs of devout pilgrims and other worshipers offering sacrifices in the Temple in Jerusalem. See in your mind's eye the huge Temple choirs with their lead singers and players of harps, lyres, flutes, cymbals, and drums standing on the steps of the Temple rousing the people to ecstatic song and dance. The psalms used in this enthusiastic Temple worship make up the Psalter we have today, which the Church uses for Morning and Evening Prayer.

A contemporary image—with perhaps a certain realistic irreverence—is a rock concert driving the screaming hordes to a frenzy with their music, dance, and lyrics. Indeed, many of these musical groups are idols worshiped by their fans because of their ability to lead them out of themselves into a kind of ecstasy. A quieter image, perhaps, would be that of a country-music star singing a sad ballad for adoring fans.

Images from Another World

The images in the psalms are drawn from primitive agricultural and nomadic cultures whose experiences are untouched by modern technology, so the analogies are somewhat distant and seem unsophisticated by our standards.

Of particular value in appreciating the psalms is a certain familiarity with the great events that shaped the national consciousness of the Old Testament people: the call of Abraham, the stories about Isaac, Jacob (named Israel), and the twelve sons of Israel. These latter went to Egypt and established the Hebrew people there, who were eventually enslaved by the Egyptians.

The psalms draw heavily on the great stories of the Exodus, beginning with Moses and his plagues in Egypt, the Passover, the crossing of the Reed Sea, the wandering in the desert, and eventually the settling in Canaan. Kings of Israel and Judah, beginning with Saul and David, were constantly conducting wars to expand their territories or to hold on to the little they had.

The next great event frequently referred to either directly or by implication is the Exile of the Jews to Babylon, where they lived from 587 to 538 B.C.E. Once restored to Jerusalem, they were never to achieve independence again. From that point on, Jewish identity was dependent on their knowledge of and faithfulness to the Law. (Psalms 78, 105, and 106 offer a poetic vision of these great events that shaped God's people, which appear again and again in the psalms we pray today.)

Finally, the images and analogies are not always clear without a basic understanding of the geography and climate of the biblical lands. For example, Psalm 126 has the line "Deliver us from our bondage as streams in dry land." The psalmist is asking God to send the rushing waters of freedom to the people, just as God sends mighty rains to flood the dried-up desert streams and turn them into raging torrents.

Likewise, Psalm 110 says, "Who drinks from the brook by the wayside and thus holds high the head." One who has never leaned down to drink from a running brook would not appreciate the power of this image. One must lift his or her head up high in order to swallow the refreshing waters that make one feel exultant on a hot day: a fitting description of the exultant Messiah.

Editing and Transmission

Our present Psalter is a collection made over many centuries in which individual psalms underwent considerable editing by different redactors. The editors came not only from different centuries but also from different theological perspectives. In some cases psalms were combined; in other cases, verses from one were inserted into others.

Furthermore, the actual transmission of the psalm texts could only be done by a large number of copyists, some more skillful than others, who sometimes made side comments on a text, called "glosses," which were later incorporated into the text itself.

Kinds of Psalms

Scholars have sought to identify general classifications of psalms based on common or shared characteristics. The identification of these divisions is the fruit of arduous exegetical efforts: working with texts in Hebrew and Greek, studying various manuscript traditions, comparing Jewish myths and rites with those of the surrounding peoples in Canaan, Egypt, and Mesopotamia. Unfortunately, although there are basic points of agreement, different scholars suggest different classifications. Their classifications are not always helpful to Christians who simply want to pray, in union with the Church, in God's own words.

A Simplified Approach

To provide the reader of the *Companion to the Prayer of Christians* with a distinct focus for each psalm, I have chosen to make my own identification for each, based on the excellent scholarship of experts in the field. This brief identification will be found in parentheses immediately after the title of the psalm.

The pages that follow offer a short reflection on each psalm used in Morning and Evening Prayer, followed by a special reflection on Night Prayer. Each reflection briefly explains the basic meaning of the psalm as it appears in the Psalter. A prayer connects that meaning with our personal lives as members of the Catholic Church. My reflections are arranged in the order that the psalms appear in the *Prayer of Christians*, beginning with Saturday, Evening Prayer of Week I (Sunday, Evening Prayer I).

When we have greater consciousness of the meaning of the psalms through the daily offering of the *Prayer of Christians*, we are able to become more aware of the movements of God's grace in our lives as God's beloved children.

Bibliography

Mowinckel, Sigmund. *The Psalms in Israel's Worship*. New York: Abingdon Press, 1967.

Oesterley, W.O.E. *The Psalms: Translated with Text-Critical and Exegetical Notes*. London: SPCK, 1962.

Lewis, C. S. *Reflections on the Psalms*. New York: Harcourt, Brace & World. A Harvest Book, 1958.

WEEK I

Sunday, Evening Prayer I

Psalm 141:1-9 (a lament by an individual)

Our lives are made up of many joys and also many sorrows; the psalms sing of both. The lament by an individual is a psalm form in which the person who suffers cries out in trust to the Lord: here, to keep the psalmist from sin and to purify his heart.

> **It has been a hard week, O Lord; many dangers threaten us. We fear what others might do to us; we fear what we might do to others. We are weak. Only you can give us strength to live righteously.**

Psalm 142 (a lament by an individual)

The psalmist is quite alone in his distress. He appeals to the Lord as if his enemies are closing in on him. If the Lord rescues him from disaster, good people will be won over to the Lord by the psalmist's witness.

> **No matter how great our suffering, Lord, you know of it. Others may fail us, may fight against us, but because you, Lord, never abandon us, your people look to the future with hope and praise your name.**

Canticle (Philippians 2:6-11)

What would it be like to be a slave, totally dependent on the whim of another human being? Becoming human was like becoming a slave to God. And more: God allowed mere humans to kill him. The Apostle Paul sang this ancient liturgical hymn with his converts.

> **O Lord, how great is the humility of Jesus to suffer even death on a cross because of his love for us. I accept my sufferings and my death as Jesus accepted his sufferings and his death on a cross.**

The Gospel Canticle at Evening Prayer: Luke 1:46-55

Mary is the mother of God because she was the mother of Jesus. Before his miraculous birth, she was a simple, unmarried virgin, outwardly of no special significance. Yet she had been chosen to be the mother of God's Son. Mary recognized her unworthiness and appreciated God's power at work in her, which raised her to such dignity. Mary recognized the greatness of her Son and, in him, appreciated God's gift to us all. For these reasons, we sing her canticle of praise each evening.

Sunday, Morning Prayer

Psalm 63:2-9 (a lament by an individual)

The psalmist is in exile from the Temple and, therefore, from the presence of the Lord. He is in an agony of loss. Yet he praises God because God loves him, even in his exile, and gives him strength and joy.

> **I, too, have departed from your sanctuary, Lord, and from the source of strength to endure the pains of life. As we celebrate the resurrection**

of Jesus, I turn to you with renewed confidence and joy.

Canticle (Daniel 3:57-88)

When the Babylonian king Nebuchadnezzar threw Hananiah, Azariah, and Mishael into a fiery furnace because they refused to worship false idols, the Lord did not let them burn. And safe in the midst of the fire, they sang this cosmic hymn of praise:

> **Lord, you created us to praise you. All the things you have created show forth your great wisdom and love. This morning we join with all creation in acclaiming your greatness and the glory of your name.**

Psalm 149 (a hymn of praise)

This psalm was especially composed to be used with music and dance in Temple worship. The people should praise God because God not only protects them but also makes them instruments of divine justice throughout the world. We are the New Zion.

> **O Lord, what a great privilege you have given me—to be one of your chosen people. As we begin the week with this song of praise, I offer you my life as a sacrifice of praise.**

The Gospel Canticle at Morning Prayer: Luke 1:68-79

Our morning canticle reveals our greatness as Christians. It was first sung by Zechariah to prophesy that his son, John the Baptist, would prepare Jesus' way. Jesus said: "Among them that are born of women, there is none greater than John the Baptist; yet the one that is but little in the kingdom of God is greater than he." We sing this canticle each morning to focus our hearts and minds on the unique gift that unites us to God, Jesus Christ. He alone saves us from our sins and enables us to live in peace.

Sunday, Evening Prayer II

Psalm 110:1-5, 7 (a royal messianic psalm)

The psalmist prophesied God's blessings on a king of Israel—his master—when he came to his throne: power to rule, priesthood, and victory. Christians realize this prophecy is fulfilled in the Messiah of Israel, Jesus the Christ.

> **Jesus, you are king for ever and ever. You are the priest of the eternal covenant. Welcome your people into your kingdom and protect us by your power.**

Psalm 114 (a hymn of praise)

This song recalls the great events by which God brought the chosen people out of Egypt and into the Promised Land of Israel-Judah: God parted the waters of the Reed Sea, stopped the flow of the Jordan River, and gave the people water from a rock in the desert.

> **What great marvels you have worked, O Lord, to form your chosen people. As members of your people, we thank you at this time of evening praise.**

Canticle (see Revelation 19:1-7)

In heaven a huge crowd sounding like thunder and the roar of the sea sang this praise of God, because the Lamb, Jesus, was united to his people in an eternal marriage.

> Lord, I too long to be part of your eternal marriage feast. You are all-powerful. Use your power to deliver me from my sins so I can be united with you forever.

Canticle in the Lenten Season (1 Peter 2:21-24)

1 Peter tells us to put up with undeserved punishment because Christ also suffered unjustly. When we suffer with Christ he forgives our sins and gives us the power to live in holiness in his resurrection.

> Your teaching challenges us, Father. Give us the grace of patient endurance so that no matter what the evil that torments us, we will grow always in holiness and love.

Monday, Morning Prayer

Psalm 5:2-10, 12-13 (a lament by an individual)

Only those who do justice by God's love at work in them can praise God in the Temple of the Lord. Awed by God's favor to him, the psalmist is confident that God will generously bless and protect those who love God.

> We ask you, Lord, as we begin this day, to lead us to act justly in all that we do. Shelter us from all those who seek to do us harm, and let us rejoice.

Canticle (1 Chronicles 29:10-13)

Because he was a warrior, God would not let King David build a temple. David's son Solomon would do that. David, however, collected the materials and generous contributions of money. Here David praises God for being so generous to the chosen people.

O Eternal God, we can give you praise and glory this morning only because you have first showered your love on us. We thank you for all your gifts.

Psalm 29 (a hymn of praise)

Ecstatic worshipers sing of God's presence in creation. A lightning storm and an earthquake remind the psalmist of God's glory. All nature displays the divine power, and yet God's mightiest feat is peace to the chosen people.

When I am in a storm, Lord, I hear your voice. Do not shatter me with your glory, nor strip me with your power. Instead, let your word bring me peace.

Monday, Evening Prayer

Psalm 11 (a psalm of confidence by an individual)

If the psalmist tries to flee from his enemies they will shoot him; instead he turns confidently to the Lord. The Lord sees all. The Lord is a refuge for the upright but punishes the wicked.

May I see your face, Lord. I tried to follow your will in all that I did this day. Keep me confident in your love always.

Psalm 15 (a liturgical psalm sung in procession)

The psalmist sings of the attributes of those pilgrims who can enter God's Temple to offer fitting worship to the Lord. Mouthing words in liturgy is not enough; worship requires holy deeds in daily life outside the sanctuary.

> Lord, I judge myself more by the prayers I pray than the service I render others. Teach me your ways of justice and mercy so I may worship you in truth.

Canticle (Ephesians 1:3-10)

This is a magnificent summary of all the gifts God has given us. God chose us before the creation of the world and made us the adopted children of God in order to bring all people into one in Christ.

> To be your children, Father of All, is to receive a gift beyond imagining. Forgiven of our sins, may we, in turn, forgive others and tell them of your love.

Tuesday, Morning Prayer

Psalm 24 (a hymn for public worship)

The psalmist asks: How can we enter into the presence of God Most High, the king of all glory? The pilgrims to the ancient Temple sing the answer: we can only pass through the gates when our pure hearts are hungry to be with God.

> Lord, I hunger for you. I am not yet all that I should be or want to be. Create a pure heart for me and make me the holy person you want me to be. I put my faith in you.

Canticle (Tobit 13:1-8)

Tobit praises God when the Angel Raphael reveals how God has been acting in Tobit's life all along. When Tobit was exiled to Nineveh, God was with him. When he was blinded, God was with him. God delivered Tobit's son from the power of evil spirits.

> **Lord, we praise you for the gifts you give us when you test us. May we always be aware of your presence as you direct all our actions during this new day.**

Psalm 33 (a psalm of praise)

Out of love God shapes the life of every human being according to the divine eternal plan. By controlling everything that happens to us God is making us into the person God wants us to be. With the psalmist we trust God and ring out our joy in song.

> **Father, we trust always in your love to bring good out of evil. May our happiness throughout the day make your Church a more perfect witness to your power and love.**

Tuesday, Evening Prayer

Psalm 20 (an intercessory/blessing prayer)

A Temple priest begins this confident prayer as his king prepares for war. The king responds that he is sure of victory because he trusts in the Lord's name. Finally, the people pray to God for the king's victory.

> **Lord, how powerful you are! Who can resist you? We put all our trust in you to guard us this night as you protected your chosen people in the days gone by.**

Psalm 21:2-8, 14 (a royal messianic psalm)

Originally, the Temple choir sang this psalm to celebrate all God's gifts to the king of Israel. We Christians identify the king here with Christ. God has anointed him to be the eternal king and blessed him with life, majesty, and glory.

How great, O Lord, is your gift to us, Jesus Christ. In union with him, as members of his body, we sing your praise and thanksgiving as we end our day in your presence.

Canticle (Revelation 4:11; 5:9, 10, 12)

This canticle is made up of three hymns sung by inhabitants of heaven in a vision given to the prophet John. The first part praises the Creator Father; the second and third parts acknowledge the glory of the Lamb who was slain but now lives.

Almighty God and Father, we join our voices with all those of your heavenly host as we offer you this evening prayer of your Holy Church.

Wednesday, Morning Prayer

Psalm 36 (a lament by an individual)

First, the psalmist describes how sin takes the place of the word of God and moves the sinner to sin. Next he praises God's love, truth, and justice in giving life and light. Finally, he asks God to shield him from evildoers.

Father, do not let sin take over my heart. Keep me free of all desires that could prevent me from honoring you. May I share the love you have given me with everyone I meet.

Canticle (Judith 16:2-3a, 13-15)

The beautiful widow Judith and all the Israelites thank God for giving her the power to cut off the head of the

Assyrian general, Holofernes, who was attacking them. We sing only a part of this long victory song of deliverance.

> **Lord of Hosts, you give us victory in all our trials. Increase our faith, Lord, so that we may see your love everywhere this day and exult in your joy.**

Psalm 47 (an enthronement song of praise)

In a prophetic vision of the end of the world, an exuberant psalmist sees that God has been totally victorious. He calls upon the whole world to celebrate with joy God's final and triumphant kingship over all the peoples of the earth.

> **Heavenly King, you have admitted us into your people and your kingdom. May everything we do this day extend your reign of love over all those with whom we work or play.**

Wednesday, Evening Prayer

Psalm 27 (a lament by an individual)

In Evening Prayer today, this psalm is divided so as to be prayed as two psalms. In the first part, the psalmist, although under attack by enemies, expects victory in the Lord and wants only to worship God joyfully. The mood of the second part is quite different. The psalmist still trusts the Lord, but his enemies grow stronger, and his prayer becomes desperate.

> **How often my troubles make me desperate for your help, comfort, and strength, O Lord. You always give me everything I need for true happiness and lasting peace.**

Canticle (Colossians 1:12-20)

God has become visible in Christ. The man Jesus, the one anointed by God, is the image of God. Everything that exists exists for him. By his death and as head of the Church, Christ brings all creation into union with our Heavenly Father.

> **In our union with Christ you make us one with you, Almighty Father. May we realize how much you have blessed us so that we can give you grateful praise and thanksgiving.**

Thursday, Morning Prayer

Psalm 57 (a lament by an individual)

The psalmist is being hunted like an animal by his enemies. He makes a confident appeal to God to defend him. When he has been delivered from his foes, the psalmist will praise God before the whole world in music because of God's great love and truth.

> **O God of Endless Mercy, how I fear the many things that can go wrong for me this day. Shelter me with your awesome power, and I will praise you morning and night.**

Canticle (Jeremiah 31:10-14)

As a punishment for their sins God allowed the Israelites to be conquered by the Babylonians; they lived in exile for forty-three years. In this joyful prophetic song Jeremiah promises that God will bring a "remnant" back to Mount Zion in a new Exodus.

> **God of Glory, our sorrows in our exile are not meant to destroy us but to prepare us for the**

greater joys that await us. Send your peace upon us as you did upon Israel.

Psalm 48 (a hymn of praise, a song of Zion)

God dwelt on Mount Zion, site of Jerusalem with walls and towers, the spiritual stronghold of God's people. This song praises God for destroying their enemies. For Christians today Zion and Jerusalem are the Church of Christ.

O powerful and saving God, we praise you for directing us in all we do today. May we witness to your justice and rejoice in the knowledge you are always with us.

Thursday, Evening Prayer

Psalm 30 (a psalm of thanksgiving by an individual)

Just when everything was going well the psalmist unexpectedly fell sick. It caught him by surprise, and he thought he would die. Then he appealed to the Lord, and God healed him. He asks us to join him in giving thanks for his rescue from death.

Lord, how often I forget to thank you for all you have done for me. Bring to mind all the gifts you have given me so that I can praise you tonight bathed in your glory.

Psalm 32 (a psalm of thanksgiving by an individual)

The psalmist tells how God delivered him from guilt-sickness when he finally confessed his sin. The wise follow the instructions of the Lord; the wicked suffer many sorrows. The one who trusts the Lord is able to rejoice always.

Lord, give me the courage to confess my sins. When I am separated from you guilt makes me miserable. When I confess my sins your grace heals me and gives me peace.

Canticle (Revelation 11:17-18; 12:10b-12a)

The seer John was given a series of visions concerning the end of the world and the ultimate victory of God and Jesus Christ, the Anointed One, the Lamb of God. In this song the Church invites even the heavens to rejoice in God's judgment and mercy.

Although we suffer the oppression of those who do evil, we know that you, O God, will bring everyone to a final judgment, rewarding the good and having mercy on sinners.

Friday, Morning Prayer

Psalm 51 (a personal confession of sin, a penitential psalm)

This poignant penitential psalm is the agonized cry of a sinner for mercy. Because sin has control over him, the psalmist cannot rejoice in God's presence, and so, confessing his sin, he asks God to give him a new heart. God hears the humble and contrite.

I, too, O Lord, am aware of my sinfulness before you. Replace my selfish heart, and make me walk secure and joyful in your path of justice.

Canticle (Isaiah 45:15-25)

Deutero-Isaiah preached this oracle in Babylon to give the Jewish exiles hope for the future: the hidden God is always bringing about divine justice through human instruments. God is revealed through God's word to save all those who believe.

> O Lord, give me the faith to trust and the wisdom to understand that you are indeed bringing me to your heavenly kingdom even through the bad things that happen to me.

Psalm 100 (a liturgical psalm sung in procession)

The worshipers sing this psalm as they enter the Temple in procession. Joy is God's gift to the people, and their happy hearts sing out their thanks in praise because God shepherds them.

> Lord, it is good to begin another day in your presence. Pour your joy into my troubled heart so that I can tell others of your goodness to me.

Friday, Evening Prayer

Psalm 41 (a lament by an individual)

Serious illness has weakened the body and depressed the spirit of the psalmist. He is anguished by a sense of personal isolation and because his enemies are using his illness to destroy him. He asks the Lord to forgive his sins, the source of his illness.

> As day draws to a close, heal me of all sickness, Lord, forgive all my sins. Enable me to forgive my enemies so I can live in peace with you.

Psalm 46 (a hymn of praise)

Christians today experience two realities: the world is in turmoil around us; God sustains us in the midst of our personal crises. This is the experience of the psalmist. He reflects on God's great works in the past and realizes that God still reigns.

> Lord, help me to be still before you so that I can hear your voice speaking to me and know that you are always with me to defend me. You are my God!

Canticle (Revelation 15:3-4)

Although we may be persecuted in this life for our belief in Jesus Christ, those who are faithful will experience final victory. We sing this canticle with the heavenly choirs of saints and angels to proclaim God's wonders and to give God praise.

> Lord, lead me to your eternal kingdom where I can be in your presence for ever and share the joy of your saints.

Saturday, Morning Prayer

Psalm 119:145-152 (a psalm in praise of God's law)

These are only a few verses from a long psalm in which the psalmist sings the praises of God's law. In God's law he finds the revelation of God's love. When we obey God's law we can be sure that God is close to us.

> To be the kind of person you want me to be will bring me joy, and to do the good things you want me to do will bring me peace. Help me, O Lord, to keep your commands.

Canticle (Exodus 15:1-4a, 8-13, 17-18) (a song of victory)

This is one of the oldest pieces of Hebrew poetry in the Bible. Composed in the thirteenth century B.C.E., it was perhaps first sung by Moses and Miriam just after they saw the waters close back over the Egyptians after the miraculous escape from Egypt.

> **What wonders you have worked, O Lord, to save your people from their enemies. Our greatest enemy is sin, which holds us enslaved. Your greatest work is Jesus Christ, who frees us from our sins and makes us holy. Thank you,** *Abba.*

Psalm 117 (a hymn of praise)

The psalmist calls not just the Israelites but everybody in the world to praise God, because God loves everybody. This brief psalm is quoted by St. Paul (Rom 15:11) to support his teaching that Christ came to bring salvation to the Gentiles.

> **We praise you O God, because your love in us gives us the strength to love others as you have first loved us.**

WEEK II

Sunday, Evening Prayer I

Psalm 119:105-112 (a psalm of mixed intention)

Containing elements of both supplication and praise, almost every verse names the Torah, or Law of God. For the psalmist observance of the Law is not oppressive but freeing: it reveals God's will, shining divine light into the darkness of human affairs.

O God, only in following your commands can I be free to love. May I always be able to discern your will for me and bask in your glory.

Psalm 16 (a psalm of trust by an individual)

Because of his past gifts, the psalmist has utter confidence that, although he does not know how, the Lord will give those who are faithful happiness forever. Peter, in Acts 2:25-28, quotes this psalm to prove God raised Jesus from the dead.

Lord, you have filled me with such joy that my heart bursts with gratitude. May I rest peacefully tonight so that tomorrow my every action will give you glory.

Canticle (Philippians 2:6-11)

The key to the Christian life is to have "the mind of Christ." This ancient hymn sung by the Christians of Paul's time reveals Jesus' mind: to become fully human and accept death. After Jesus had humbled himself, God exalted him as Lord of the universe.

Only when I accept my human inadequacies, Father, can I be one with you and with your Son, Jesus. May everybody see your glory in the humility of my life.

Sunday, Morning Prayer

Psalm 118 (a processional hymn)

In a jubilant procession to the Temple, worshipers sing: when all seems lost, the Lord works marvels to save the people, so praise God. Jesus quotes this psalm (Matt 21:42) to show that God made him the cornerstone of the new creation.

Lord Jesus, I call upon you in my weakness and suffering because I am confident that you will rescue me from all my sorrows by your resurrection.

Canticle (Daniel 3:52-57)

When the Babylonian king threw three young men into a fiery furnace because they would not worship his golden statue, God sent an angel to protect them from the flames. From the midst of the fire they praise God's name, glory, kingship, and greatness.

As we begin this day, O Lord, we ask you to protect us from the fires of evil so that we can

**join your holy people throughout the world
in praising you.**

Psalm 150 (a song of praise)

This musical hymn of praise concludes the Book of Psalms. We do not just praise God in church; we give our praise in the world God made and in which God is constantly acting. God's greatness is everywhere and always.

Conscious of your gifts and guidance, each day we praise you, Lord God, but especially on this day when we celebrate the resurrection of your Son, Jesus Christ.

Sunday, Evening Prayer II

Psalm 110:1-5, 7 (a royal messianic psalm)

The king's own prophet spoke this oracle when his master was enthroned. The king's power comes from God because he is God's "son." He will be victorious over his enemies and intercede for his people. Jesus is the "Master" of this psalm (Matt 22:44).

Lord Jesus, you are our eternal high priest before God, Your Father. May we share in your victories this day as you shatter all the satanic forces seeking to draw us from you.

Psalm 115 (a hymn of praise)

The psalmist compares the all-powerful God of Israel with the useless pagan idols. God blesses all those who fear and put their trust in God. In turn, we praise God for giving us life.

Lord God, we join all the peoples and all the heavenly hosts in praising you for the glory of your name. All truth and love come from you to transform our lives.

Canticle (see Revelation 19:1-7)

The myriads of heavenly hosts sing this canticle before the throne of God. They invite us to join in their praise. The Lamb, Jesus, celebrates his wedding to his bride, the Church, as the saints achieve final victory by their good deeds.

Lamb of God, our earthly voices unite with those of heaven as we celebrate your victory over Satan and his angels. Your love unto death enables us to give you glory forever.

Canticle in the Lenten Season (1 Peter 2:21-24)

This early Christian hymn professes our faith in the innocent Jesus as the Suffering Servant of his people. Jesus takes our sins upon his cross so that we can bear up under all our sufferings, whatever form they take, in union with him.

Lord Jesus, unite all our sufferings of body and pain of heart to your pierced heart. By our union with you on your cross may we lead others to union with you in your resurrection.

Monday, Morning Prayer

Psalm 42 (a lament by an individual)

Far from God's Temple, the psalmist is persecuted for his faith in God. In extreme anguish, he longs to be able to worship God freely once again. Even though God seems to have forgotten him, he still praises God because God is always his savior.

> How often I feel so distant from you, my God. Increase my weak faith so that even in my most severe trials I am conscious of your consoling strength.

Canticle (Sirach 36:1-5, 10-13)

When God punished the chosen people in the Exile, God showed his holiness. In this canticle Sirach prays that God will show glory by delivering Jerusalem from its enemies and restoring the unity of Israel. Christians call on God to protect the Church.

> We begin another day in your service, Lord of the Universe. Help us to do great deeds of love in your name so that all the nations of the world will know your holiness.

Psalm 19:1-6 (a hymn of praise)

Our morning celebration closes with an ancient hymn that borrows heavily from Babylonian sun-god worship. The psalmist, however, praises God as the creator of the entire universe, including the sun itself. There is no God but our God.

> Father, as the sun passes through the sky to warm us and give us light, we think of the warmth and light of your Son, Jesus, who brings us to the glory of your kingdom.

Monday, Evening Prayer

Psalm 45 (a royal psalm)

The court poet sings this psalm to his king on the day of the king's wedding to a foreign princess, acclaiming the power of the king and the beauty of his bride. We thank God for the marriage of Jesus to us, his Church.

> **Lord Jesus, you are the bridegroom of our soul. You adorn us with the gift of holiness. Guard us this night so that tomorrow we can do the good acts our holiness requires.**

Canticle (Ephesians 1:3-10)

From all eternity God has chosen us as adopted sons and daughters. God has freed us from the lusting power of our sins so that we can live wisely in praise of God.

> **We praise you, Father, for your gifts. May our kindness to others witness to your mercy so that everyone will want to come to unity with us and your son, Jesus.**

Tuesday, Morning Prayer

Psalm 43 (a lament by an individual)

Oppressed by his enemies, the psalmist asks that God guide him into the divine presence by sending forth light and truth. No matter how bitter the present moment, the psalmist lives in confident hope that God will bring him joy.

> **God our Savior, guide us this day to do your will. Even though our enemies may do evil to**

us, we will never do evil to them. Instead, we
will bring even our enemies with us to your
altar of praise and thanksgiving.

Canticle (Isaiah 38:10-14, 17-20)

This "Canticle of Hezekiah" is the prayer of a good
king of Israel who, as he lay dying, was tormented that
his life was over. But the merciful God extended his life.
For his life, the king praises and gives thanks to God.

**Lord, death frightens all of us. Many see only
an abyss of darkness after death. Yet we know
that even when we die we shall live for ever,
because you have promised us eternal life in
Jesus Christ.**

Psalm 65 (a hymn of praise)

The psalmist looks upon God as an all-powerful king
who calls the chosen people to dwell in God's Temple,
Zion, where God forgives their sins. Then the psalmist
praises God for the magnificence of creation and the loving care with which God tends it.

**God our Savior, as we begin our day, we join
our voices of praise with those of the Church
throughout the centuries. We experience your
awesome power and beauty for ourselves, and
so we shout for joy and sing.**

Tuesday, Evening Prayer

Psalm 49 (a Wisdom psalm)

The psalm singer arrives at an insight into the futility
of riches. They keep the wealthy from growing in true wis-

dom of life, and the wealthy cannot take their riches to their graves. But God will redeem the life of the one who is just.

> **Oh God, how great are the temptations of this world to trust in ourselves and build up earthly treasures. Free us from all greed, teach us our limits, and give us the grace to serve others in humility and detachment.**

Canticle (Revelation 4:11; 5:9, 10, 12)

In a vision of heavenly glory, the prophet John heard three hymns sung by the hosts of heaven. They make up this canticle. Our canticle praises God, creator of all things, and Jesus, the Lamb whose death purchased us to serve God.

> **Lord Jesus, you died on the cross so that we might reign gloriously with you. Keep us free from sin this night so that we might give you glory and praise tomorrow.**

Wednesday, Morning Prayer

Psalm 77 (a lament by an individual)

The psalmist feels God has abandoned him in his great crisis. Things are not like they used to be; God worked wonders in the past. Why not now? Implicit in this prayer is confidence that God will soon work wonders again.

> **We read about the miracles you performed in Scripture, O Lord, yet we still experience so much distress and grief. Give us confidence in you. Work new wonders for us, Lord.**

Canticle (1 Samuel 2:1-10)

The barren Hannah sang this exultant canticle after she finally had a child, Samuel, the great prophet of the Old Testament. She rejoices in the absolute power of God, who always acts for the good of those God loves. Mary's *Magnificat* praises God for the same reason.

> **Great is the mystery, O Lord, that you have all dominion, and yet we are free. Use our freedom and your power always to bring about the coming of your kingdom of joy, peace, and happiness.**

Psalm 97 (an enthronement psalm of praise)

This psalm glorifies God as king of all the earth, a king of great power, as storms and earthquakes reveal. Most of all, God is a just king who takes care of those who are just, defending them against all evils. We rejoice in God's glory.

> **Lord God, king of the world and of our hearts, we praise you for having revealed yourself to us in your Son, Jesus Christ. May our witness today bring the whole world to acknowledge you as king.**

Wednesday, Evening Prayer

Psalm 62 (a psalm of confidence)

Rich, lying, and powerful enemies are attacking the psalmist. Yet God is his refuge, sheltering the psalmist by the divine power of love. As a result, the psalmist is standing firm, with peace in his heart.

> Father of all love, we too are attacked for our ideas and beliefs, and we do not always respond in love or with trust in you. If you repay us only according to our deeds we have no hope; but we trust in your mercy this night.

Psalm 67 (a thanksgiving psalm at the harvest festival)

The psalmist praises God for the fruit of the harvest. At the same time, he asks God to continue to bless the chosen people so that all the peoples of the earth will join in praising the giver of all good things.

> Our Father, may the works we did today bear witness to your goodness, kindness, and justice. May our lives always reflect your own holiness, so that everyone who knows us will know you are our Father and theirs.

Canticle (Colossians 1:12-20)

Jesus is the cosmic head of all creation and incarnate head of the Church on earth. By dying on his cross, Jesus brought us into union with himself so that everything in heaven and on earth might be at peace. This hymn thanks the Father.

> Gracious God, it is easy to rest in peace this night because you have given us over to the care of your Son, Jesus. May we rise tomorrow refreshed and ready to serve.

Thursday, Morning Prayer

Psalm 80 (a national psalm of lamentation)

The northern tribes Ephraim and Manasseh, sons of

Joseph, and the tribe of Benjamin are all under attack. God seems to have abandoned them. The psalmist prays to God to protect the vine (God's very own people) that God has planted in this land.

> **Shepherd of my Soul, oftentimes we, too, feel so overwhelmed by the trials of life that we think you have abandoned us. But you are only using our trials to teach us the ways of your righteousness. Renew our trust in you!**

Canticle (Isaiah 12:1-6)

The psalmist (not Isaiah) has been rescued from a serious difficulty, so now he praises the Lord. He calls upon Israel to proclaim God's mercy to all the nations. Jerusalem is the city of Zion, where God, the Holy One of Israel, dwells.

> **O Holy God, our savior, your Son Jesus dwells with us, your Church. Today may our hearts be full of praise and thanksgiving for your many favors to us. How great you are!**

Psalm 81 (an enthronement psalm of praise)

On a great feast day, a sacred Temple rite celebrates God's covenant with the chosen people. The Lord speaks in this psalm to call the people back to full obedience to the law. If they return, God will give them victory over their foes and bountiful harvests.

> **Father, do not let us turn away from your law this day. Help us to recognize and be thankful for the wisdom of your teachings. May we always live according to your will in love.**

Thursday, Evening Prayer

Psalm 72 (a royal psalm)

This psalm was written by a court poet on the accession to the throne of a new king of Israel; Christian tradition sees the Messiah. Jesus is the king who fulfills all the demands of justice and mercy. He provides for his people, defeats their enemies, and answers the cries of the poor and helpless.

> **You have poured forth your blessings into our lives this day, O Lord. We thank you. May we give to our fellow human beings the same justice, mercy, and care you have given us. May we all be one in your eternal kingdom.**

Canticle (Revelation 11:17-18; 12:10b-12a)

Seven angels stand before God. When the seventh angel blows his trumpet, the twenty-four elders sing the first part of this canticle. The last two strophes announce the victory of the saints after Michael defeats Satan, the primeval serpent.

> **We praise you, Lord, with the entire court of heaven, for you have begun your reign in our lives. We look forward in confident hope to your final victory over all evils.**

Friday, Morning Prayer

Psalm 51 (a personal confession of sin, a penitential psalm)

Deeply conscious of his sins, the psalmist cries out to God for mercy. Only God can create a pure heart for him and fill him with holy wisdom. The psalmist's sorrow for his sins is a sacrifice of praise, which the Lord will accept.

> How often, O Lord, do we resolve to give up sin and lead holy lives, and how often we fail to keep our promises! Rescue us from the power of our evil desires so we can be free to love others this day.

Canticle (Habakkuk 3:2-4, 13a, 15-19)

The prophet Habakkuk knows that ultimately the powerful and compassionate God will save the people from their oppressors. No matter how difficult life is, the prophet will continue to trust God, who gives him the strength to endure and even flourish.

> When things go wrong in our lives, O Lord, and we are filled with fear and anxiety, give us the confident assurance that you gave Habakkuk. Today show us you are present, directing and strengthening us.

Psalm 147:12-20 (a hymn of praise)

The psalmist urges Zion to praise God, who protects the chosen people and gives them peace. By God's all-powerful word the universe is ruled in an orderly and wise manner. Most of all, only to the chosen people has the Lord revealed God's laws and decrees.

> Lord, we, the New Zion, praise you for your gift of peace in Jesus Christ. May we share your word with those to whom you send us this day: family, friends, and co-workers.

Friday, Evening Prayer

Psalm 116:1-9 (a psalm of thanksgiving by an individual)

When the psalmist was about to die, he cried out to the Lord, and the Lord heard him. When he was absolutely unable to help himself, the Lord delivered him from danger. The greatest thanks for our salvation is to walk always aware of God's nearness.

> **Many have been the sorrows of my day, O Lord, and yet I have survived them all to praise you in this evening song. Shelter me tonight so that I can rise in the morning to continue to serve you by serving others in Jesus' name.**

Psalm 121 (a psalm of trust)

Originally this psalm was sung as a dialogue between pilgrims ascending the Temple steps and the Temple singers. The pilgrims seek God's help; the singers assure the pilgrims of God's constant protection on their journey of faith.

> **Today we are on our journey of faith, and so we ask you, Guardian of Pilgrims, to direct our steps to the heavenly Jerusalem and to protect us from all who would lead us astray or deter us from our goal.**

Canticle (Revelation 15:3-4)

Those in heaven are so filled with joy at God's victory over all the evils that afflict the world that they break out in constant hymns of praise and thanksgiving.

> **We join our voices with those of the hosts of heaven and the whole Church on earth to praise you, Father, for all the gifts you have given us this day through your Son, Jesus.**

Saturday, Morning Prayer

Psalm 92 (a royal psalm of praise)

The anointed king praises God, who has given him victory over all his foes. Although the wicked may flourish briefly, ultimately they will not last. But the just will bear rich fruit even into old age and will live in the presence of the Lord.

> **Lord, no injustice will go unpunished; no evil will escape your wrath. May we dwell in your court in heaven where the saints will live forever. Lord, have mercy.**

Canticle (Deuteronomy 32:1-12)

At the end of his life, Moses sings of God's power and justice and especially of God's kindness to Israel in making it God's very own people. At the same time, Moses rebukes the people for not having been faithful to the God who saved them.

> **Lord, Great God, you have chosen us, your Church, as your special heritage. Keep us faithful to your commands and fulfill your promise of eternal life.**

Psalm 8 (a psalm of praise)

In one of the most beautiful psalms, the psalmist is filled with wonder at the magnificence of the heavens, in awe over frail humans. Only a great, all-powerful God full of love could create such human and natural splendor.

> **Father, Creator of All, may we see your own radiance in things you have made. May we see the attractiveness of your Christ, Jesus, in all whom you put in our paths today.**

WEEK III

Sunday, Evening Prayer I

Psalm 113 (the first of the Hallel "praise" psalms)

This psalm, along with Psalms 114-118, was used at the great Jewish feasts: Passover, Tabernacles, and Weeks. The Lord himself sang these at the Last Supper. It honors God for the divine power and great mercy to the most miserable and humble of us.

> **Hallowed be your name, Father. In the midst of our suffering you give to the most barren all that we need for peace and happiness in this life and in the world to come.**

Psalm 116:10-19 (the fourth Hallel "praise" psalm)

Delivered from a great danger, the psalmist offers a libation in the Temple as a public act of worship. He vows to serve the Lord before all God's people. Our lives are our thanksgiving sacrifice before the world.

> **Most Gracious God, we Christians see "the cup of salvation" fulfilled in the Eucharist, and "vows to the Lord" sacramentalized in baptism. May we always be your servants, for we have put all our trust in you alone.**

Canticle (Philippians 2:6-11)

We Christians are called to live united to Christ and to one another. Humility is essential in preserving our communion with one another because pride causes factions in community. The key is to be like Christ. In humility we share the lordship of Jesus.

Lord Jesus, give me the gift of being like you in mind and heart. May I be as humble as you were on your cross so that I may reign with you and give glory to your Father.

Sunday, Morning Prayer

Psalm 93 (an enthronement psalm of praise)

The psalmist praises the awesome, eternal majesty of God, who rules the universe in wisdom and holiness. Even the powerful surging seas and their roaring waters are nothing compared to the glory of God. God rules everything by everlasting decrees.

Lord, we praise you for the beauty of creation. We can live only because you have given all of nature to nourish us. In a world threatened by human misuse of your gifts, may we always respect the things you have created.

Canticle (Daniel 3:57-88)

We also sang this hymn at Sunday, Morning Prayer, Week I. In the heart of the fiery furnace, the three young men call upon all creation—angels, inanimate things, all living things, and the servants of the Lord—to praise and give glory to its creator.

When we look at the endlessly varied and complex things you have made, O Lord, we know you are truly great because you love the beauty you have made. May we always respect and reflect the beauty of your creation.

Psalm 148 (a hymn of praise)

This praise-psalm is an orderly exhortation for all creation to praise the one true God. Sun, moon, stars, sea monsters, birds, and mountains have all been called gods by other peoples. The psalmist knows they are not gods; our God created them all.

Lord of All Wonders, you not only are creator of all things, you mercifully draw us, your servants, near to you, and you share your Spirit with us, through Jesus Christ.

Sunday, Evening Prayer II

Psalm 110:1-5, 7 (a royal messianic psalm)

The Letter to the Hebrews (5:6-10) uses this psalm to prove that God anointed Jesus to be the high priest of the New Covenant. Jesus learned obedience through his sufferings; as a result, he became the source of salvation for all.

O High Priest of the Eternal Covenant, we unite our sufferings of this week to yours. Offer up prayers and entreaties on our behalf so that we can be with you forever in the heavenly kingdom of your Father.

Psalm 111 (an acrostic hymn of praise)

This psalm praises God, not for God's works of creation but for God's works of salvation. God has saved the chosen people and given them a covenant of justice and truth: a share in divine wisdom, which lasts forever.

> **Lord, you have established us, your people, in wisdom. As we begin this week, may we witness to those still in the darkness of sin the joys of living justly, truthfully, and compassionately.**

Canticle (see Revelation 19:1-7)

Alleluia means "Praise Yah" or "Praise Yahweh," God's personal name "I Am," revealed to Moses from the burning bush. We join the heavenly hosts in singing this inspired canticle to celebrate the marriage feast of Christ with his Church.

> **Lord, we live in the midst of trials that sorely afflict us. Only our certainty in your final victory sustains us. We sing "alleluia" because our God is king.**

Canticle in the Lenten Season (1 Peter 2:21-24)

That the Church keeps repeating this canticle during Lent shows how important it is to endure opposition patiently and to love those who hate us. In this way, we share the sufferings of Christ and grow in holiness.

> **During this Lenten Season, Father, may our example of patience and kindness lead all peoples to a knowledge of your truth and a love of your divine law.**

Monday, Morning Prayer

Psalm 84 (a hymn of praise)

Pilgrims sang this ancient hymn as they went up to the great Feast of Tabernacles. Weak with longing to be in the Lord's house, they gained strength as they drew nearer to their goal. The Lord will reward the innocent and give joy to those who love God.

God our Shield, strengthen your pilgrim Church. May it be a source of salvation for all who come to it. May we, your people, witness to others in love.

Canticle (Isaiah 2:2-5)

Some seven hundred years before Christ, Isaiah prophesies universal peace for the world in this compassionate oracle. All the world will be attracted to God, and God's word will be proclaimed in Jerusalem. God's justice will bring an end to war.

Today, Heavenly Father, your word goes forth from the Catholic Church to convert hearts so that all nations will be able to abandon war and work for peace.

Psalm 96 (an enthronement psalm of praise)

Awed by God's wonders as creator, ruler, and judge, the psalmist is impelled to sing this magnificent hymn glorifying the majesty of God. He summons the Israelites and the whole world to praise God as king over all earthly kingdoms and above all false gods.

You have established your kingdom among us, Heavenly Father. It is a kingdom of peace,

justice, and truth. May we live in your kingdom forever with your Son, Jesus Christ.

Monday, Evening Prayer

Psalm 123 (a lament by an individual)

Slaves are completely dependent on their masters and mistresses, whose hands reward or punish, give or strike. Our claim to God's mercy is our complete helplessness before God and our need for protection against the scorn of the rich and powerful.

> **O Merciful Master, how filled with pride I am, wanting to "do it myself" so that I can "be somebody" on my own apart from you. Give me the humility that opens the floodgates of your kindness toward me.**

Psalm 124 (a psalm of thanksgiving)

The psalmist describes how God has delivered the chosen people from their powerful enemies, who otherwise would have overwhelmed them like a river at full flood; God has freed them from their enemies' traps. An overwhelming sense of relief characterizes this psalm.

> **O Lord, I know how often I have escaped disaster only because you freed me. As evening falls I recall your mercies to me this day and praise you for your gifts.**

Canticle (Ephesians 1:3-10)

God loves us and so has made an amazing plan for us. God's plan is to adopt us as children in Christ Jesus so we can be holy and happy. God can accomplish this plan perfectly because God is all-wise and all-powerful. Praise God's mercy!

> **Loving Father, I unite myself totally to your plan for my salvation. May every one of my actions be in harmony with your plan so I can give you glory before your people.**

Tuesday, Morning Prayer

Psalm 85 (a lament by the community)

When God forgave the people, they rejoiced. Now more troubles have come, and the psalmist cries out for renewed outpouring of divine mercy. Finally, the psalmist sings a prophetic promise of prosperity, justice, and peace to those who fear God.

> **O God, how often you have saved us from disaster, and for this we praise you as we awaken to serve you again. Keep us in truth, love, and union with your Son, Jesus.**

Canticle (Isaiah 26:1-4, 7-9, 12)

Isaiah prophesies peace for all who enter into the strong city protected by the Lord. The human heart hungers for such peace but rarely achieves it. God gives this great gift to those who turn to God in confidence and live in justice.

> **Great God, help your Church bring justice to a world awash in war and to human hearts broken by conflict. Restore peace to our families and society so all may sing your praises.**

Psalm 67 (a psalm of thanksgiving)

God saves the human race by revealing to it the right ways of living in justice: first through Israel, today through

Christ's Church. God's creative acts in the world continue as God blesses the earth and makes it bring forth fruit.

> Father, we praise you for having given us the power to witness to your love through the holiness of our lives. May all the peoples join us in praising you, O Lord.

Tuesday, Evening Prayer

Psalm 125 (a psalm of trust)

Jerusalem was built on Mount Zion, surrounded by other mountains. God protected Jerusalem so that evildoers would not lead the just into sin. The psalmist asks God to bless the good, punish the evil, and give God's people peace.

> Guard us, O Lord; you have made your Church the New Zion. Keep it safe from all evils, and give us the power to forgive from our hearts all who harmed us this day.

Psalm 131 (a psalm of trust)

A great gift from the Lord is to be content with the simple things God gives us instead of straining for more. The psalmist is intensely aware of his own weakness and the Lord's power. Relying on God instead of ourselves gives us true peace.

> Heavenly Father, even though we may achieve worldly success, may we realize that all the good things we have and accomplish are your gifts.

Canticle (Revelation 4:11; 5:9, 10, 12)

The Church joins heaven in worshiping Jesus, the Lamb of God. By shedding his blood he has gained the right to open the scroll containing God's plans. The Lord God and God's Christ will rule over all creation for ever and ever.

> **Father, we praise you this evening for having brought us to the close of another day as your beloved children.**

Wednesday, Morning Prayer

Psalm 86 (a lament by an individual)

This psalm is packed with human emotions. The psalmist fears, hungers for God, trusts in the Lord, thanks for past rescues, is confident of future ones, praises God's greatness. He appeals for signs of God's love, God's strength and consolation.

> **I have given myself to other gods in the past, O Lord: money, comfort, security, success. Now all these have deserted me, and I can only call out to you for mercy.**

Canticle (Isaiah 33:13-16)

The prophet speaks in God's name to tell of the kind of life required to enter God's sanctuary and so be filled with God's blessings: do only good, speak the truth, refuse evil allurements, do not even listen to tales of violence.

> **Teach us your truth, O Mighty God, and free us from all greed and love of violence. May we receive your Son, Jesus, in the Holy Eucharist: our daily food and drink.**

Psalm 98 (an enthronement psalm of praise)

The enthronement of a king was a momentous event in Israel because God's anointed could rule God's people with justice and lead them to victory. In this psalm God is enthroned as the king, not only of Israel but of all the nations.

Heavenly Father, we acknowledge the kingship of your Son, Jesus. May he reign in our hearts this day, leading us through the darkness of this world to eternal life in your heavenly kingdom.

Wednesday, Evening Prayer

Psalm 126 (a psalm for the harvest festival)

The Lord had delivered the chosen people from bondage before, and they sang and laughed. Now, once again, they experience a new bondage. Farmers plant seed fearful that the harvest will be poor; when it is abundant, they sing for joy. So will it be in the new freedom.

At the close of this day, O Lord, we sing our thanks for the gifts you have given us. May the cares of this life, no matter how oppressive, never turn our hearts from confident trust in your kindness and mercy.

Psalm 127 (a wisdom psalm)

Without God's active intervention in our lives, all our efforts are useless. The psalmist sees sons as arrows protecting their father in the conflicts of life. God's gift of the family still provides protection for all its members.

O Lord, as we fall asleep in your presence tonight, let us see your hand in all that we have

accomplished this day so that we may praise you with this Wisdom song.

Canticle (Colossians 1:12-20)

How awesome is the Christ we worship by obeying his commands and by eating his Body and Blood! Even the angels were created through him and for him. Yet he lowered himself to die on a cross so that we might live in peace with God and one another.

Almighty God, may we appreciate more fully the gift you have given us in Jesus. May we keep his commands so that we can grow in our knowledge of you and be united with you for ever.

Thursday, Morning Prayer

Psalm 87 (a Zion hymn of praise)

Because God dwelt in his holy Temple on Mount Zion, it is called the City of God. Christians know Zion was the foreshadowing of the Church, the true mother not just of the neighbors of ancient Israel but of every nation.

Lord Most High, you send us forth this day to witness to your fatherly love for all men and women of every race, nation, and culture. Through us, extend your kingdom to the ends of the earth.

Canticle (Isaiah 40:10-17)

This oracle reveals that the God who comes to us as a shepherd taking care of his lambs is the all-powerful creator and sustainer of the universe. He is without beginning or end, is answerable to no one, and rules all peoples as he wills.

> **Lord God, our frail human minds cannot comprehend your power and majesty, and our pride-filled hearts cannot always accept the generosity of your love. Guide us this day to the everlasting pastures of your joy and peace.**

Psalm 99 (an enthronement psalm of praise)

This psalm reminds us vividly that God is a king to be feared, who rules justly all the earth and its peoples. In divine justice, although God forgave Moses, God punished even that great prophet by excluding him from the Promised Land. Bow down before God!

> **Lord, we acknowledge your awesome kingship over us. May everything we do bear witness to your own holiness. May we keep your laws and forgive others as you have forgiven us.**

Thursday, Evening Prayer

Psalm 132 (a royal psalm of praise)

God had dwelt in the Ark of the Covenant during the Exodus from Egypt to the Promised Land. Christians see the Lord's oath to David in this psalm as fulfilled in Jesus. Jesus is God's anointed, of David's stock, who establishes the new covenant.

> **Lord Jesus, you need no Ark to bring God to us. True God and true man, you dwell in our tabernacles throughout the world and give yourself as our bread and wine. May we share your victory over sin and death.**

Canticle (Revelation 11:17-18; 12:10b-12a)

After the seventh angel blew his trumpet in John's vision of the end of the world, all the heavenly hosts sang this canticle to celebrate God's victory. Those who lived holy lives on earth in union with Jesus share in this great triumph over Satan.

> **Lord Jesus, we have no victory in our personal battles against sin except the victories you give us when we put our trust in you. May we live with you for ever in your kingdom.**

Friday, Morning Prayer

Psalm 51 (a personal confession of sin, a penitential psalm)

This psalmist's depth of sorrow for sin is unique in the Old Testament. All sin is against God, and only God can forgive sin. The psalmist turns to God in confidence that in divine mercy God will give him a new heart and a new spirit of innocence.

> **Reveal my sins to me, O Lord, so I too can turn to you with a contrite spirit and humble heart and receive from you the gift of forgiveness and everlasting life.**

Canticle (Jeremiah 14:17-21)

When the chosen people in the Old Testament were being formed, God used natural disasters and wars as punishments to teach them to follow the commandments. Jeremiah proclaims the destruction of Jerusalem as God's punishment and asks for God's mercy.

> **O Lord, we too deserve your punishment for our sins, but in your mercy you have given us**

your only begotten Son, Jesus Christ, to intercede for us and obtain forgiveness. Lord, have mercy. Christ, have mercy.

Psalm 100 (a processional hymn of praise)

Originally sung by Israelite pilgrims as they entered the gates of the Temple, this song invites everyone and everything to join in their praise of the merciful and faithful God.

As we begin our day in your service, we ask you to keep us free from sin and all evil so that we might praise you with renewed joy.

Friday, Evening Prayer

Psalm 135 (a hymn of praise)

This liturgical psalm sung in Temple worship recalls the great deeds for which God deserves praise: God governs all nature; God led the people out of Egypt; God conquered for them the Promised Land. False gods can do nothing at all.

Today, Father, you give us all the advances of science so that we can know you better from your wonders in nature. You give us your Son, Jesus, to lead us to our heavenly home.

Canticle (Revelation 15:3-4)

This triumphant "Hymn of Moses and the Lamb," sung in the courts of heaven, reveals that God not only performs astounding deeds, God works them according to divine justice and mercy. All the world will eventually worship the Lord, God Almighty.

> **Lord, your gift of faith to me reveals the great deeds you have done in my life. I close this day singing with Moses and the angelic hosts of your great holiness and love.**

Saturday, Morning Prayer

Psalm 119:145-152 (a psalm of mixed intention)

In this section of the long psalm praising the law of God, the psalmist cries out at daybreak to God to give life by revealing God's laws. Today, Christians know that God's law is his love for all peoples. When we obey it, it brings us justice and peace.

> **Lord, we can gain happiness and eternal life only by living out in our own lives your law of love. You have sent Jesus Christ to teach us your law and the Holy Spirit to give us the power to keep it. We praise you for your gifts!**

Canticle (Wisdom 9:1-6, 9-11)

The Book of Wisdom infers that King Solomon offered this prayer asking for the gift of wisdom to rule his people. Eternal Wisdom knows all things and has glorious power. She is God's gift to guide all human affairs.

> **Lord Jesus Christ, you alone are the true Wisdom of God, for you are the Word made flesh. You continue to dwell among us by your powerful teachings and your presence in the Holy Eucharist. May we always live by your wisdom.**

Psalm 117 (a psalm of praise)

This shortest of the psalms is perhaps only a fragment of a longer psalm. It is an ardent call to praise God because of God's love and faithfulness to our welfare.

Amen, Lord. Again, we say, Amen.

WEEK IV

Sunday, Evening Prayer I

Psalm 122 (a song of Zion)

How exciting it is to plan a trip, especially a pilgrimage, and then to be actually there. To be standing in Jerusalem where the Lord lives in the Temple moves the pilgrim-psalmist to pray for the object of his love: on Jerusalem, peace.

> **Lord, we too love your house and your dwelling place: the Holy Catholic Church and the tabernacle of the Holy Eucharist. Strengthen your Church so it can extend your peace to the ends of the earth.**

Psalm 130 (a lament by an individual)

Deep in the human heart God has planted a longing for God. The psalmist gives voice to this craving we all have for innocence and freedom from guilt. Confident of the Lord's mercy, the psalmist can now only wait for the Lord to forgive.

> **Be merciful to us, Lord, for you are the Lord of mercy and forgiveness. We acknowledge our sins of this day and ask for your forgiveness and a night of peace.**

Canticle (Philippians 2:6-11)

Humility is the bedrock of the spiritual life; without it no one can advance in holiness. Even Jesus humbled himself in order to be exalted by the Father: from being God to being human, even to die. With St. Paul and his Churches we praise the Risen Jesus.

How great is the mystery of suffering and death, Lord Jesus. But you drew back the veil of fear when you embraced death for yourself so that you could give life to us. Help us to embrace your death and live your life.

Sunday, Morning Prayer

Psalm 118 (a processional hymn)

Exuberant crowds of worshipers carrying branches sang this hymn as they processed at the joyful harvest festivals. Lines from the hymn are used by Matthew (21:33-46) to attest to the messiahship of Jesus. Once rejected, he is now the cornerstone.

Every Sunday is a harvest festival for us, O Lord. By your death you have harvested us in order to fill us with your own Body and Blood at the sacred altar of the Mass.

Canticle (Daniel 3:52-57)

To bless is to make holy by invoking God's favor on a person or thing; it also means to honor or give glory. It is used in the latter sense here. We bless God because of who God is and what God has done in creating the world and making of us a chosen people.

On the Sunday feast of the Resurrection, we bless you, Father, for having raised Jesus to

your right hand in glory. May we be united to
the Risen and Exalted Jesus forever.

Psalm 150 (a song of praise)

Music and dance played a more important role in the enthusiastic Temple worship than in our Catholic services. This concluding hymn of the Psalter is calling upon the Temple dancers and a whole orchestra to praise God's holiness and powerful deeds.

I praise you, O Lord, with the instruments you have given me—your graces at work in my mind and heart. May my whole being praise you as did the being of Mary.

Sunday, Evening Prayer II

Psalm 110:1-5, 7 (a royal messianic psalm)

God rules all of history. Where pagans see only coincidence and luck in human events, the psalmist sees God working out the divine plan through human agents, especially kings and priests. We Catholics see it all summed up in the Lord Jesus: priest, prophet, and king.

Lord Jesus, intercede for us with your Father; speak your word to us in your Church; rule over our lives by the gentle movements of your Holy Spirit.

Psalm 112 (an acrostic wisdom psalm)

"Virtue is its own reward" does not apply here. The psalmist sees that God blesses the devout and holy person with the good things of life. The wicked are punished. The revelation of retribution beyond the grave comes later in Jewish theology.

> O Lord, give your favor to those who put all their trust in you. Bless them in this life and reward them with the joys of your eternal kingdom.

Canticle (see Revelation 19:1-7)

Again the Church sings with the heavenly choirs, praising God with the liturgical praise used in the Old Testament: "Alleluia!" This is the time to celebrate God's victory over evil with feasting on the Holy Eucharist: Christ himself.

> The table you spread for us on earth, O Lord, the Body and Blood, Soul and Divinity, of Jesus Christ, perfects us to celebrate the eternal feast in your heavenly kingdom.

Canticle in Lent (1 Peter 2:21-24)

By accepting all our sufferings as a way to follow Christ, we become more sensitive to the evil of sin in our lives. At the same time, we become more responsive and compassionate to others who suffer.

> Father, you made us for life and happiness, yet our lives are filled with pain and sorrow and end in death. Give us the grace to grasp the mystery of suffering and death. May Christ's wounds heal our wounded nature.

Monday, Morning Prayer

Psalm 90 (a lament)

The poet recognizes the eternity of God and acknowledges God's absolute power. In contrast, our lives are short and filled with pain. The poet knows, however, that God can give us wisdom to understand life's mysteries and joy to bear life's sorrows.

> In our modern world, O Lord, we are surrounded by death and suffering, yet so often they lead only to rage and hopelessness. As we begin this day, give your Church the power to share your wisdom and so to give all peoples hope.

Canticle (Isaiah 42:10-16)

See the prophet on the Temple steps singing this new song. He calls all the peoples to join him in celebrating God's victories. God, like a warrior, will destroy his enemies and lead the helpless into safety by straight paths.

> Lord God, we are so surrounded by the things human hands have made that we cannot see your works. Help us to see your victories over evil so we can sing this new song with your entire Church.

Psalm 135:1-12 (a hymn of praise)

We pray only part of Psalm 135 today, focusing on God's waging war on behalf of the chosen people. It was written in a violent age, and without wars the Israelites could not have possessed their land. They know the value of God's victory and so they praise God.

> O Lord, we too live in a violent age with wars going on in all parts of the world. Empower us to win the victory of peace by proclaiming the gospel of your Son, Jesus Christ.

Monday, Evening Prayer

Psalm 136 (the Great Hallel)

In Temple worship a solo singer or choir sang this hymn and the worshipers supplied the repeated response. It celebrates God's mighty works—first, of creation, and then, of salvation: from the Exodus to the entry into the Promised Land.

> **Lord Jesus, we sing the hymn you sang when you praised your Father at the Last Supper and left to your disciples the Great Remembrance: your own sacred Body and Blood given up for us in your sacrifice of Calvary.**

Canticle (Ephesians 1:3-10)

For the fourth week in the *Prayer of Christians,* the Church has us give praise for the gifts God has given us, the adopted children of God: wisdom to understand and holiness to live God's plan for our salvation: to bring all peoples into unity under Christ.

> **Send your Holy Spirit upon us, Father, that we may reflect during the night on the mysteries you have revealed: your eternal love for your children and the forgiveness of our sins through Jesus Christ.**

Tuesday, Morning Prayer

Psalm 101 (a royal psalm)

This psalm was sung by the king upon his accession to the throne. Perhaps he sang it each year in a festival. It is the king's "inaugural address" of promises to the Lord of the way he will rule the Lord's people.

> By baptism we share in the kingship of Christ, and so we too make the promises of this psalm to you, O Lord, morning after morning.

Canticle (Daniel 3:26, 27, 29, 34-41)

One of the three young men thrown into the fiery furnace of Nebuchadnezzar, Azariah offered this prayer of a national confession of fault. Recalling God's past promises to Israel, Azariah asks God to be merciful to those who trust in God.

> Heavenly Father, because of Jesus' once-and-for-all sacrifice on Calvary, we have no need to offer you animal sacrifices. Instead we unite our hearts to those of your Son, who offers you the perfect holocaust of praise.

Psalm 144:1-10 (a royal psalm)

Perhaps this was first sung by King Hezekiah (716–687 B.C.E.) when he asked God to give him the strength, as God had strengthened King David, to lead his people in their battles against their enemies.

> Protect your people, O Lord, in our struggles this day against those who will try to harm us because we seek to live according to your will.

Tuesday, Evening Prayer

Psalm 137:1-6 (a lament of the community)

Homesickness is a painful experience, as any child knows. The poet recalls how his heart ached when he could not worship God properly in exile. He curses himself should he ever forget Jerusalem. Without hand or tongue he could not praise God in song.

Jesus has revealed that "true worshipers worship the Father in Spirit and in truth" (John 4:23) anywhere and anytime. And so, Father, we worship you now and in this place, which Jesus makes holy by his presence.

Psalm 138 (a psalm of thanksgiving)

There are times in our lives when others overwhelm us with kindness, and our heart swells with appreciation. The psalmist has experienced such kindness from God when God gave him courage. In perseverance, he has known the glory of the Lord.

Lord, we do not expect instant solutions to all our problems, for they are many and severe. But in all our troubles you give us courage and a way out. Thank you, God.

Canticle (Revelation 4:11; 5:9, 10, 12)

Heavenly hosts praise God endlessly, and they rejoice in God's presence as we do on earth when we are in the presence of the ones we love. This canticle captures the reasons for the experience of joy.

Lord Jesus, we experience on earth the fruits of your death. You have arranged all events according to your eternal plan so that we might enter your kingdom and be happy with you forever.

Wednesday, Morning Prayer

Psalm 108 (a composite psalm)

Made up of Psalms 57 and 60, the first part thanks God, and the second part contains a prophecy of victory over

Moab, Edom, and the Philistines. At the end, the psalmist cries out for help because only God can give Israel victory over its many enemies.

> **We wake and praise you this morning, O Lord, confident of the many victories you will give us in our battles big and small because you always do what is best for us.**

Canticle (Isaiah 61:10–62:5)

Taken from The Book of Consolation, Deutero-Isaiah prophesies a new age for Zion, an age of saving justice and salvation that all the nations of the world will witness. Catholics recognize this is a prophecy of the Church, and so the Church sings for joy.

> **Father, we are gathered in the New Jerusalem celebrating our marriage to your Son, Jesus Christ. He is the bridegroom, the Church, his bride. Let the marriage feast be one of great joy!**

Psalm 146 (a hymn of praise)

The poet has an extremely perceptive insight into the workings of God in ordinary human affairs. God is not a ruler from afar but the Lord who daily tends to the needs of the weakest of children.

> **How many motives your inspired poets give us for praising you, O Lord of All Creation. Give us the grace to recognize your loving dominion in all we do this day.**

Wednesday, Evening Prayer

Psalm 139:1-18, 23-24 (a lament by an individual)

One of the most passionately personal and spiritually powerful psalms in the Psalter, it is the favorite of many. The psalmist is overcome by God's intimate knowledge of his innermost being and overwhelmed by God's constant presence and care.

> **Not only are we your creatures, O Lord, made in your image and likeness, you have raised us up to be your adopted children through Jesus Christ. Help us always to recognize your fatherly and unselfish love in all that happens to us.**

Canticle (Colossians 1:12-20)

The lot of the saints that we share is to walk in the light of Christ, to be forgiven our sins, to have peace within ourselves, and to live in peace with one another. Great is the power of the cross on which Christ shed his blood that brought all this about.

> **As our day comes to an end we turn to you, Lord Christ, to give you thanks for your gifts. May we be humble as you are humble, and therefore share in your exaltation to eternal glory.**

Thursday, Morning Prayer

Psalm 143:1-11 (a lament by an individual, a penitential psalm)

We live in a world that teaches self-reliance; for the psalmist everything depended on God. We live in a world that is highly competitive; the psalmist was hounded by enemies. To have peace we need what the psalmist sings here: trust in God.

> Lord, our God, we gather to thank you for having protected us during the night, and we ask you to continue to protect us during the day. Do not let our sins overtake us or separate us from your loving hand.

Canticle (Isaiah 66:10-14a)

Childhood memories of a mother's warm, cuddling, and loving body inspire this oracle. The prophet calls us to rejoice and be glad because we are God's children, and God will fondle us and feed us from the breast of the New Jerusalem.

> How hard it is for us, Lord, to believe that you love us as much as you say you do. Yet when we put our trust in you and rely on your love, we live in peace and our hearts rejoice.

Psalm 147:1-11 (a hymn of praise)

The all-powerful God, who governs the course of nature, deserves our praise. But in addition, God heals the most wounded and the most humble and punishes evil, and delights in those who trust in God's love. Let us sing to the Lord and give thanks.

> Lord, I am among those most wounded and most in need of your love. Show me this day that you really are guiding me and protecting me. Give me the gift of trust so I can praise you with a joyful heart, free from all anxiety.

Thursday, Evening Prayer

Psalm 144 (a royal psalm)

This one psalm is broken into two prayers at Evening Prayer today, which reflects the opinion of many scholars that Psalm 144 is really two psalms. We prayed the first part earlier this week on Tuesday, in Morning Prayer. Today's second psalm sings about the wealth of the nation when its king is victorious: strong and beautiful children, lots of food, successful farming, happy people. And all these are gifts from God.

> **We have known victory, O Lord, when we follow your ways and obey your commands. We give you thanks for the blessings of this day and ask you to continue to rule and protect us as your beloved children in Christ Jesus.**

Canticle (Revelation 11:17-18; 12:10b-12a)

A great day of reckoning will come when the evil in the world is definitively and finally overcome. This promise of decisive judgment and lasting reward heartens those who struggle to live a good life in spite of the many allurements to sin.

> **Father, we thank you for the assurance you give us in Christ Jesus always to protect us in the battles of this life and to reward us in the next.**

Friday, Morning Prayer

Psalm 51 (a personal confession of sin, a penitential psalm)

As it does every week, Friday Morning Prayer begins with this profoundly moving confession of sin. The psalmist is crushed by guilt but turns humbly to God for forgiveness and for a new and clean heart so that he in turn can bring others back to God.

> **Sometimes, O Lord, I am so filled with fear for my sins that I cannot even admit I have sinned. Send your Holy Spirit upon me so that I can honestly face up to and confess my wrongdoing, confident of your merciful forgiveness.**

Canticle (Tobit 13:8-11, 13-15)

The Book of Tobit reveals God's secret workings in the lives of those God loves. God works wonders in the New Jerusalem, the Church, and so the Church sings this beautiful song of thanksgiving, which tells of Jerusalem's "forever" joy.

> **Lord God, you are truly the great king over all the earth. We praise you as we seek to draw all people to join us in offering you fitting praise and thanksgiving.**

Psalm 147:12-20 (a hymn of praise)

The psalmist exhorts the people to praise God, first, because God defended the city; next, because God governs all nature; finally, because God governs the chosen people by his word. The Church is God's people: we are the new Jacob and live in the New Jerusalem.

> **We praise you, O Lord, as our day begins. Help us to see your powerful works this day in our lives and to live more fully by trusting your word more unswervingly.**

Friday, Evening Prayer

Psalm 145 (an acrostic hymn of praise)

We join the psalmist in praising God, because each verse reveals the wonders God works for each of us. True to God's promises, God has been compassionate and loving; God has supported us and raises us up; God fulfills our desires and gives us justice; God protects and saves us.

> **O Lord, I praise you for your miracles in my life. You have revealed yourself to me again this day, and so I pray to you this night. Increase my faith, especially when I find my cross too heavy to bear.**

Canticle (Revelation 15:3-4)

Only in heaven will we be able to sing this hymn as God deserves to have it sung. Yet even on earth, by living in God's word we already have some inkling of God's glory, which will be our glory for all eternity.

> **Truly ravishing and awesome are your works, O Lord God Almighty! May our lives reflect your grandeur on earth so that we can sing this canticle before your throne in heaven for ever and ever.**

Saturday, Morning Prayer

Psalm 92 (a psalm of thanksgiving)

In his joy at knowing God, the king-psalmist sees that because fools cannot discern God's plan they will be destroyed. The good flourish and bear fruit, praising God for giving them the strength to live honorably and to witness to God's truth.

> Hear our morning prayer of praise, O Lord. In spite of suffering we are filled with joy because we know you will reward those who do good. Give us the grace to be just.

Canticle (Ezekiel 36:24-28)

Speaking in the person of God, the prophet proclaims one of the greatest truths in revelation: we are able to live according to God's law only because God has given us a new heart.

> All creation praises you, O God, but especially the new creation of your chosen people. We praise you in song, but mostly we praise you with our entire lives of holiness.

Psalm 8 (a psalm of praise)

To appreciate the teaching of this psalm, go outside on a dark clear night and look at the stars; then come in and look in the mirror. Yet God loves us more than the stars! Praise God!

> When I see myself, Father, I do not see greatness; yet you made me in your own image. How loving you are: to make me like you! Make me more and more perfectly like you each day, in Jesus' name.

PSALMS FOR NIGHT PRAYER

Canticle (Luke 2:29-32)

When Simeon held the infant Messiah in his own arms he experienced in a single rhapsodic moment the joyous end to the centuries of waiting and yearning that Israel and its prophets had endured. What peace for believers! What joy to the world! What glory to God!

Each day, Lord Jesus, we can hold you in our hands. Each day we can proclaim you to the world. Each day we can give your love to others through our lives. We sing with Simeon of your mercy.

Sunday, Night Prayer I

Psalm 4 (a lament by an individual)

Like ourselves today, the psalmist lived among people who did not believe in God and did evil simply to gain material success, thinking it would bring them happiness. The Lord God gives joy of heart and blessed peace to those who turn to God in trust.

We sing of your mercy to us, Father of Lights. Although you may not have given us great

wealth, you have kept us from being overcome by anxiety. Help us always to seek your truth and live according to your justice.

Psalm 134 (an invitation to praise)

Addressed to the priests of the Temple, the psalm exhorts them to worthy service of worship. The psalmist, perhaps the high priest himself, then blesses the other priests, and in so doing empowers them to offer fitting praise through the long night of vigil.

When you bless us, O Lord, we can do all things in your name. Protect us this night; may we recall your gifts to us today, so that we may praise you all the more tomorrow.

Sunday, Night Prayer II

Psalm 91 (a psalm of trust)

The psalmist enumerates the evils that can come upon a person at any time: morning, noon, or night. Enemies attack; diseases kill. But angels will safeguard those who put all their trust in the Lord. They will know God is with them always in majestic power.

Emanuel, God-with-us, protect your Holy Church during the darkness of the night. As the sun rises bringing new light, may your Church proclaim your saving truths with new power so all may enter under the protection of your love.

Monday, Night Prayer

Psalm 86 (a lament by an individual)

The psalmist is a poor person who has been devoted to the Lord and who is now undergoing serious opposition. In the past God has healed him, so in this new crisis, not knowing how to respond, he asks the Lord for guidance and a sure sign of God's protection.

> **Lord, I too am conscious of your many favors to me, especially those of this day. I put all my trust in you for the future because your Son, Jesus Christ, died for our sins and was raised to glory, which he shares with us.**

Tuesday, Night Prayer

Psalm 143:1-11 (a lament by an individual, a penitential psalm)

What is unusual about this psalmist's desperate appeal for help is that he knows he has sinned. But he knows how God has done good to sinners before. Therefore he appeals confidently and asks God to teach him to obey God's commands in the future.

> **Lord, I too have sinned, and I have no right to your help in the trials of my life. But you are a forgiving God of love and compassion, so I too call upon you to keep me safely in the paths of your justice and love.**

Wednesday, Night Prayer

Psalm 31:1-6 (an appeal for protection—a lament)

The psalmist is caught in the coils of oppression, and there is an urgency to his appeal for help. He makes his entreaty confidently because God is a God of justice who shelters and directs those who seek refuge in God.

> **Tonight, I, too, commend my spirit into your hands, Lord Jesus. You redeemed me from my sins and will keep me on the straight way of peace, justice, and love.**

Psalm 130 (a lament by an individual)

Tormented by his sin, the psalmist pleads to God. He does not actually ask for forgiveness (perhaps he does not feel worthy enough even to ask), but he knows the Lord does forgive. He simply cries out his longing and trusts the Lord will act.

> **Forgive my sins I have committed this day; heal all your people of their sins. Strengthen your Church, and let us sleep in peace to rise to serve you in the light of a new day.**

Thursday, Night Prayer

Psalm 16 (a psalm of trust by an individual)

How happy is the psalmist! The Lord has given him everything: a love for others, constant guidance day and night, physical health, and even the assurance he will never know decay. He is fully happy now and will be forever. Happiness in God alone!

> **Father, your people share the experience of the psalmist. We know all our happiness comes**

from you. Help us to share our happiness with others by the witness of our lives.

Friday, Night Prayer

Psalm 88 (a lament by an individual)

This poet is experiencing an agony of mind and body that is unrelieved by any hope, unique in the Psalter. It is his hopelessness that is most distressing. Could he be a leper, blind and excluded from all society, already living his own death?

Lord Jesus, it is for such as this suffering psalmist in the depths of despair that you became one of us. By your death and resurrection you offer even the most miserable new life on earth and happiness in heaven. Praise Jesus!